The Luckiest Dog Not Alive

ISBN-13: 0692873791

Book & Cover Design: Xavier Bertolotti

Illustrations: Don Gibbon

SUVETAR PUBLICATIONS
GLOUCESTER, MASSACHUSETTS

Eppy

For my father, Ralph Hendrickson who, by being deaf, taught me how to listen.

The Luckiest Dog Not Alive

One dog's journey into the afterlife

Cynthia Hendrickson

Dogs' lives are too short.
Their only fault, really.

-Agnes Sligh Turnball

Preface

The Luckiest Dog Not Alive is about my dog Eppy, who lives a wonderful life, one Milk Bone at a time and then passes on. Sound familiar? Not fun, is it? But you should know that this is a book with a very happy ending.

This story imagines the emotions and experiences of Eppy after death from his viewpoint, as opposed to how a pet owner feels after the loss.

Eppy and I moved into my childhood home to take care of my dad in 2007. My mother had recently died and he needed help. Dad was 82 years old and 100% deaf. He lost his hearing from a WWII shrapnel wound.

My dad first looked at Eppy with skepticism. My parents (my mother mostly, it was her house after all) weren't pet people and Eppy was the first dog to show up at the front door in sixty years. Since my father couldn't sign or read lips, we communicated with a whiteboard and a dry erase marker. His first look at Eppy was less than welcoming.

"What are you planning to do with that dog?"

"Well, he's mine so I guess he'll have to stay with us," I said using the whiteboard.

"Does he bark much?" Dad quizzed, pretending to be serious.

"You're a real comedian," I wrote.

From that point forward, the three of us thrived together as friends and cohorts. Eppy played outdoors with me and never left "Grandpa's" side when indoors.

Eppy and I lived with my father for the last eight years of both of their lives. They each died in 2015 – Eppy on Valentine's Day weekend, and my father just a few days prior to Christmas. If I owned a truck and it had died that year, my life would have been prime material for a sad country song.

Losing Eppy was one of the deepest sorrows of my life and my father was heartbroken at the time as well. But losing a dog is not just about you or me. What about the dog or cat or other family pet? Shouldn't we be concerned about what has happened to him or her? Of course we should!

As soon as I started worrying about what was happening to Eppy, I stopped thinking about my terrible loss.

Wasn't it my job to now be concerned about him, the same way he always went out of his way – at least if he didn't have to move – to make sure I was happy?

How about if he stopped eating? Just refused steak tips, left over lobster claws, perhaps other favorite foods? What if Saint Somebody offered him a treat and he responded, "No thank you, sir, I'm too depressed to eat." What if that same saint said, "Well, my fine friend, why don't you just go take a swim in that lovely ocean over there and I'll have someone come over and toss you a few tennis balls?"

And Eppy responded, "Thanks anyway, but I'll just lay here and stay out of everyone's hair and perhaps lose a few pounds in the process."

Not eat, stay out of the way, *lose a few pounds in the process???*

Then I began to imagine how Eppy made the transition from here to "there" and found both new friends and old and wrote this story.

Yes, this is serious stuff, but stop sniveling. Put that box of tissues away. Read on; soon you'll be able to smile and recall the many fond memories of your own dog.

Here's Eppy. His "portrait" is still hanging on our kitchen wall. When friends visit and notice it, they inquire, "Wow, who did that portrait of Ep? It looks just like him!" Yes, it does look *exactly* like my 106-pound Lab/Newfoundland mix rescue dog. But it's just a print that I bought for $12.99 at Marshalls.

This is his story....

Prologue

It feels so good not to be sick. I believe I may have caused quite a scene. I certainly wasn't being melodramatic; this was real. Thought I'd die.

Eppy looked around him; something was clearly different.

Where am I? Why is it so bright?

Eppy became even more confused when he heard a voice directly above him. He raised his eyes. "Can you please provide us with a description and explanation of yourself?" the voice said.

A pen dropped down to Eppy and he caught it with his right paw. What followed was a blank page. Another page drifted down and the inscription read: "Write no more than 150 words about yourself."

I'm not sure why I can comprehend speech or read or even catch a pen from the sky. How could I even know what a paper and pen are?

Before Eppy had a chance to start writing, he heard more voices but their speech was garbled. Then he plainly heard this:

"It's OK canine, we found some background data on you. Please take the following and proceed to Gate A23 for further instructions."

Once again, a paper slowly glided down to him. It floated, weightless and free. When it was within Eppy's grasp, he caught it and proceeded to read. Here's what it said:

Hi, my name is Eppy. I am a rescue dog from West Virginia.
I was adopted at age two by a woman as her running partner.
What was she thinking? I am 106 pounds of solid lard: A Black
Lab/Newfy mix. Lucky for me, my human lives with her
soft-hearted father. He gives me three Milk Bones a day and
table scraps. Half a cheeseburger or several steak tips
on a good day.

I thought I was the cat's meow – pun intended – until my
human met a guy skiing. She decided that I needed an "alpha dog."
Why can't I be my own alpha dog? "Boyfriend" thinks otherwise.
Thanks to "Boyfriend," I am not supposed to drink out of puddles,
eat food from the table, or get treats unless I deserve them.
Like I'm supposed to earn a Milk Bone? Grandpa won't ever allow
that to happen.

Despite this setback, I wouldn't trade my life here for all the Milk
Bones in China. That's a lie. Everything else is true.

Another paper followed this one. Eppy regarded it
with dismay.

SPECIES: CANINE

STATUS: TBD

IMAGE:

Panic set in. Eppy raised his eyes to where the voices were coming from and yelled, "Do you suppose I could rewrite this? It was written seven years ago, I didn't even write it myself! I can't write or talk or read. At least I didn't think that I could. My life has changed since that time. I'm a much better dog! Just look at me. Do I look anything like that dog in the photo?"

I'd better not.

Buddy wrote this for some magazine. She thought it was a riot. Like that photo is funny? If I really look like that, I'm in big trouble. Can't believe that she made a reference to lying here. Not to mention the sarcasm.

"Take your paperwork and proceed as directed. Good Luck."

Gulp.

Heaven goes by favor. If it went by merit, you would stay out and your dog would go in.

-Mark Twain

I must be in the right place. The sign just to the back left of where I stood announced: PARADISE IS OPEN TO ALL OF GOD'S CREATURES. Whew! Being a dog, I am reassured. I do recall the phrase now. Pope Francis, our newest pope, was credited with saying just that to a little boy whose dog had just died. This pope even took his own papal name from the patron saint of animals, Saint Francis of Assisi. It's confirmed: Animals can go to heaven. Truthfully, how could a creature who was named DOG (backwards for GOD), not have a chance to experience a jubilant afterlife? With pricked ears, I bound forward.

I come to an abrupt stop when I see a man sitting on a plush gold chair. His hair is a wavy white; he has a white beard as well. He's wearing a full length purple robe, covered by beige material that looks like a bunch of sheets just thrown around him. There is a circular gold glow surrounding the back of his head. He is barefoot. When I notice the long brass key tied to a sash on his left side, I become confused. Is he holding the key to Paradise?

He studies me in silence. He is pensive, but after several moments, his solemn expression turns into a warm, convivial grin.

"Welcome to your afterlife, Eppy. I am Saint Peter, and it is my pleasure to meet you."

Before I can reply, Saint Peter continues, "You are a fine-looking specimen of a canine, Eppy. Regal looking. Majestic." Saint Peter winks at me. "I'll bet you were a big hit with the ladies."

Saint Peter's comment catches me by surprise, I'll admit. I was, of course, admired by many women. Only one was extraordinary. Such a shame for the "powers that be" to decide to transfer me here. I made the most important woman in my world break down in tears today. My earthly rock became totally unhinged. I had anticipated her being distraught, but didn't think she'd become hysterical and make it even more painful for me to have to leave her.

"Well, sir," I stammer, "the canine female sort didn't seem to notice me, but human women found me well-mannered and pleasing in appearance. I had a regular day-to-day relationship with one special female, plus I knew all of her friends." I look shyly down at the ground.

"You don't need to address me as 'Sir' my dear dog." Saint Peter says. "We are going to be friends, and I want you to think of me as being your equal." Suddenly, Saint Peter looks directly past me, frowning.

"I'm sorry to have to tell you this, but your 'special female' doesn't look very happy presently."

How could Saint Peter know what Buddy was doing?

"What is she doing?" I panted.

"Do you really want to know?" Saint Peter questions, his soft tender face now fraught with concern.

No. "Yes, of course," I reply.

"Buddy is sitting alone in the driver's seat of her vehicle. She has her arm around a green paper bag and is staring down into it. Buddy is 'talking' into the bag that, as I zoom in closer, contains an exquisite brown wooden box. Apparently, your earthly remains are in that box, along with a 'Rainbow' poem and a 'Death Certificate'. You are considered a 'Beloved Family Member'." Saint Peter smiles approvingly.

A beloved family member? I am so proud and flattered. I raise my possibly muddy paw up to meet Saint Peter's hand. I feel a kinship with him already.

My joy quickly dissipates as I think back to Buddy sitting alone in the car with all that was left of the earthly me. Holding back tears, I sit still and try to hide my feelings.

"She'll be fine, Saint Peter," I say. "Buddy has a flair for the dramatic." There is probably not much confidence in my voice. As I speak, I can just picture Buddy lying on the floor in a fetal position, clutching my filthy, drool-soaked blanket, eyes glued on my photo prominently displayed on our mantel. Couldn't I just sneak back down there and dig her a hole to lay in until she feels better? Perhaps I should ask?

"Ah, Saint Peter, since we are working on being friends here, I was wondering if I could ask you a small favor. Could you possibly – I realize that this is a stretch – give me a pass to go home for, say, an hour or so? If possible – again, please let me know if I'm pushing the envelope here – think you could let me keep this human voice while I'm there? If I could explain how delightful this place is and tell her about you…Well, Buddy would be relieved to say the least."

Saint Peter rolls his head back and howls with laughter, "You are a card, my dear dog."

Then Saint Peter becomes somber.

"Look, Eppy, I know that you are going to miss your previous life. Loving anyone involves eventual loss. It's what makes us human. Or dog in your case."

Again, I offer my paw to Saint Peter and he gently pats me.

"Hey, cheer up my boy. Eppy, you'll see Buddy again. You will need to be patient and strong. Remember how everyone used to say, 'He has a mind of his own' when referring to you? We can help you get that spirited mind set back intact. You'll see. Don't fret."

We both become still. The two of us stand enclosed by a whiteness, the only actual color coming from Saint Peter's clothing. I am no longer in any physical pain, yet I am devastated by an ache in my chest that hurts even more. I can't help myself. I hang my head in despair. I am homesick.

"I'm sorry, Saint Peter," I say. "It seems to be my time to be melodramatic. Please let me try to explain:

"You see, life for me on Earth wasn't a blank page. It was full of color, and smell, movement and people. I swam in the saltwater of the ocean, languished in the clean freshness of a mountain stream. Running was a joy, and I'd jump in pure ecstasy when I saw Buddy lace up her running shoes.

"She was reluctant to run at first but then my eagerness became contagious to her. We'd splash through puddles, let the rain drench us and the wind ruffle us.

"When we were done, we'd both drink cold water, sit on the front steps and rest. There's a feeling called peace and I think that's what we experienced.

"My customary schedule, unlike Buddy whose behavior was more erratic, was my life's contentment. I reveled in my routine. Each morning began with a tender awakening. This loving woman, my Buddy, would walk unhurriedly down our front staircase. She would wrap her robe tightly around her if it was cold or remove a layer in the heat of summer. We both preferred the cold. My tail would wag like crazy when I spotted her! I had no control over its strength – I was just ecstatic to see her.

"She'd greet me with, 'Good Morning, my sweet angel.' (See, Buddy was already convinced I would go to Heaven.) 'Did you sleep well?'"

"Like I've ever had a problem with that."

"'Grandpa will be right down to give you a Milk Bone.' She'd pat me then head off to the kitchen to get a cup of that steamy hot drink with the strong aroma.

"About this time, I'd hear a rather loud mechanical sound from the top of the back staircase. It was Grandpa coming down on his stair lift.

"Grandpa was already elderly (All three of us disliked that word.) when I arrived seven years ago.

"Dog years go by too fast and I caught up with him in age rather quickly. Our arthritic conditions were similar which bonded us. The fact that he was my official 'dispenser of all treats' certainly didn't hurt our relationship."

"Grandpa said the same thing every morning. 'Hi Eppy boy. What a good boy!' He'd then reach over to his stash of Milk Bones and hand me one. I would gently take it out of his hand.

"He was impressed with my placidness, as were those mini humans we often had visiting.

"I knew it was important to everyone that I was passive. Besides, why bark when you can just sigh? Over exertion was not part of my lifestyle.

"The days were always joyful—sunshine, rain, sleet, or snow. Weather did not affect me. I would swim in the ocean in all four seasons. Sometimes I would just sit and watch the world go by, letting the waves roll over me.

"On winter weekends, we drove a very long time to get to the mountains. Sitting in the back of a vehicle was not exactly my favorite thing to do. There were lots of happy people there, always laughing and drinking out of big red plastic cups or clear round crystal ones with long stems. My nickname at our mountain home was 'The Big Lump'. It made them laugh, so it was fine by me.

"If you went by human standards, I suppose at 106 pounds, I was large on the dog spectrum. I was, still am I think, a mix of Black Lab and Newfoundland; bigger and better of course than a small dog. Not that I was ever conceited, Saint Peter, just self-assured, I suppose. Grandpa and I were always told that we were handsome. No one ever said that to Buddy, but in my mind, she was handsome as well."

Thinking about my past makes me even more forlorn. Do dogs have tears in the afterlife? I didn't want them—it was distressing enough to watch humans hurt that way. I couldn't break a heart by having a loved one see me in such a state. I pull myself together.

Heaving a sigh, Saint Peter speaks and brings me back to present time. I was always a big day dreamer, so I wasn't surprised that I had my head in the clouds, so to speak.

"Please give me more information as to what you believe caused your demise." says Saint Peter. His voice is almost a whisper; his face expresses concern. How gracefully he can change the subject! Not that this one is particularly a pleasant topic for me.

"Yes, Saint Peter. I will tell you as much as I can remember." I am indeed grateful that this strong and thoughtful saint has taken me under his arm, or wing perhaps.

"It was a Friday, and I was going to Maine to celebrate Valentine's Day with Buddy and her boyfriend who came into our lives four years earlier.

"He thought he was the 'alpha' dog in our pack. I was my own alpha dog and wanted him to remember that."

"Sorry, Saint Peter, I don't mean to sound arrogant but they don't say 'you can't teach an old dog new tricks' for nothing.

"Don't get me wrong, Alpha Boy is my pal. We just had fun kidding around with all this 'I'm the boss' stuff. I consider Alpha Boy part of my family, too.

"Well, my stomach felt queasy all the way up to the Maine house. Aside from being nauseous in the car and later vomiting on the living room rug, my other health concerns began to surface. My breathing was shallow; my legs seemed to feel as though 50-pound weights were attached to them, my chest ached, and my eyes were runny. I never understood the expression 'sick as a dog', but I knew that I was a dog. and that I was sick. Very sick.

"Buddy didn't know what to do. She was crying as she spoke on the phone to someone.

"I overheard things like 'rice and boiled chicken,' 'plenty of water'. Alpha Boy brought her a jacket, and they proceeded to leave the house and drive away. Most likely they were driving to pick up supplies for me, I being their top priority now.

"Shortly thereafter, the pains got worse. I was in panic mode. What was that line that Grandpa used to say?

"I know, it was from reruns of an old television show. A man covers his hands tightly over his heart, considers the sky and moans, 'This is the big one, Elizabeth!' I felt the same ache in my chest. This was my 'big one,' I realized.

"If my heart were in any better condition, it would have broken into thousands of little pieces. Worse than dying was the realization that I would never see Buddy again. It was inconceivable to imagine not being with her.

"I must truly admit, I loved Buddy more than life itself."

"After what seemed like forever, Buddy and Alpha Boy came through the door. Alpha Boy went into my room first and said, 'He's dying, honey.'

"No, he's *not*. Pick him up and let's get him to the hospital *now*.

"Alpha Boy awkwardly lifted all 106 pounds of me. If I had any strength at all, I would have cracked up laughing! He is such a 'goober'. I just loved some of the vocabulary I picked up from her friends.

"Guess it wasn't that funny because he dropped me into the back of his vehicle like a sack of potatoes. I landed with a thud. Talk about kicking a dog when he's down. I'm sure Alpha Boy meant no harm. He was scared, too.

"Buddy got into the front seat with her now concerned partner.

"Alpha Boy kept saying, 'Talk to him; talk to him! He needs to know you're here!'

"Half praying, half cursing, Buddy climbed over the seat and pulled me to the area just below her chest. I always loved when she did that.

"There were times when I was so sad or so lonesome for Buddy that I thought my meaningless life had ended. This time, it was happening for real.

"I tried to wag my tail for her, not one of my better efforts, but it did in fact rise and then, slowly and painfully, it dropped. That is my last earthly memory."

"I believe that my heart just gave out, Saint Peter. You probably know that I am *old*. Older than dirt, as the humans like to say."

His next question is, "Did you see a tunnel with a white light coming through it?"

"Like in the movies?" I smile momentarily.

Saint Peter returns my smile. "I know it sounds silly, but there actually is a tunnel that connects us to your home. It's like a shooting star. Some see it, and others don't."

Saint Peter changes the subject. "How good are you at listening and following directions?" *Saint Peter has a lovely face*, I thought to myself.

"Excuse me? Oh, um, until I went deaf several years ago, I was a very good listener."

"Ah, yes, God does add some difficult tests of fortitude in what humans term The Golden Years."

"Well Saint Peter, it didn't really seem all that important to Buddy that I learn to do some things, but I never strayed far from her."

"You are full of the devil," Saint Peter says.

"I am?" I gasp.

"Just an expression, Eppy, just an expression."

Amused by his own joke, Saint Peter snickers, "We both know that you prided yourself on how much you could get away with. Weren't we just discussing the phrase 'He has a mind of his own?' It certainly was difficult for Buddy to keep up with you after her accidents. God knew that you stayed by her side."

"Did God know?" I ask.

I lower my head and stare sadly into my front paws and proceed to relay this story to St. Peter.

"Buddy broke her leg two years in a row doing something called skiing. I never actually saw 'skiing' per se, but obviously, it is some sort of activity involving height because when we drove up to the house in Maine, there were snow-covered mountains.

"Buddy could no longer ski after her second accident. No offense, but perhaps after the first break, when she smashed her femur in half, Buddy should have considered another sport."

"This worked out in my favor; she would hang around the house with me all day while Alpha Boy skied with his pals. His loss, my gain. Belly rubs and extra Milk Bones. Spa Days."

Buddy and I always had such a good time, I thought to myself. *Where would I have ended up if Buddy hadn't gone to that adoption event and rescued me?*

I'm no idiot, I knew to do the "paw thing" (i.e., I yanked her into me and wouldn't let her go, a look of pure pleading in my eyes.) Buddy got sucked into that right away.

I held onto her for dear life. She looked very athletic and having dark eyes myself, I was blown away by her dazzling blue eyes. It was a match made in heaven; just an expression. I obviously don't understand heaven, since for the time being, it looks as if I'll be hanging out here with my new pal Saint Peter.

"Hey, Saint Peter, would you like to know how Buddy and I got our names?" I beam. This is a funny story.

"Of course," Saint Peter responds. I can tell that he is pleased to see me becoming cheerful.

"You see, I once lived in a very warm area with a family that didn't want me. They barely fed me, never gave me treats and eventually sent me away. I went to a colder place which was fine with me. In both places, I was called, 'Buddy.'

"One day, I was brought to a big yard with a bunch of puppies. These puppies were all together, but I was left alone. This was disconcerting to me until two women came over and looked down at me. The shorter one said, 'Wow – that is one handsome dog.'

"The other woman replied, 'We are getting a dog for me, not you. I need a smaller dog, one that will stay with me when I go running. Besides—look at that drool. Yuck.'

"I have to admit, it was in the summer and warm weather and I aren't the best combination.

"'If you want my opinion that is the best dog *ever.*' Her pal got that right.

"The decision-making woman frowned in resignation and said, 'Fine, I'll take him.' All the humans there cheered, and off we went to my new home.

"'What should I name this dog of mine?' my worried new owner pondered. 'I wonder what Theo will think of him? Can two dogs live happily together in the same neighborhood?'

"Nobody had told me that another dog would be in the picture. His name was Theo?

"'Buddy is a stupid name for a dog—so generic. Guess some people in West Virginia have no imagination.' Was it me, I wondered, or did my new owner have some issues here?

"Luckily, her face now beamed. She was smiling! 'I've got it. Theo Epstein is the new 'boy wonder' for the Boston Red Sox. We have a Theo; now we'll have an Epstein.'

"We can call him 'Eppy,' which sounds close enough to 'Buddy' so that he won't be confused. That's it. Settled!'

"No one was going to argue with her, Saint Peter. Talk about having a mind of your own, ha-ha. Just then I came up with my own brainstorm.

"If this woman was going to take my name away from me, I would give it to her. She has been 'Buddy' to me ever since then. Humans call her something else, but they can do their own thing. I was pleased that I gave her a pet name."

"That's a very nice story," Saint Peter is obviously pleased to see my change of attitude.

"May I offer you a drink?"

He motions to a line of water bowls just across the
room.

"Thank you, Saint Peter."

I walk over to a line of multi-colored water bowls situated on the right side of our meeting area. I select the fawn colored one; it was the shade of the coat of a good canine pal of mine, Gucci.

She was an elegant little thing; with a name like that, who wouldn't be? She was tough to compete with when it came to being dainty.

I would splatter water everywhere (which is why I had to drink it outside in the summer time and with a zillion paper towels under it in the colder weather.)

Now, trying my very best not to slobber, I lap the water quietly and purposefully. My success at this effort makes me smile. I can even smile now! Gucci would have smiled, too.

Feeling more at ease, I yawn, stretch, then in my old habitual way, I circle several times and drop to the ground in front of Saint Peter.

"Saint Peter, can you please tell me what happens next? I know I'm a big dog, but I do get frightened sometimes. I mean, I'm not even sure where my next bowl of Beneful is coming from."

"Certainly, Eppy, I just want you to relax and get comfortable with me." Saint Peter spread his arms out and his cloak looks like it now had wings. *Is he an angel?* I wondered.

"Eppy, my sweet dog, I am going to escort you to your final resting place. It's not a 'resting place' because you will get to run and play. You'll be able to jump onto sofas and you will even have an ocean to swim in."

An ocean! I run and jump; my arthritic legs are free of pain. I am young again. "That's great news! You are the best, Saint Peter. I owe you one for all of this."

"No, honorable dog, you deserve all of this. You were loved by others, and you loved and cared for your family. You fulfilled your duties and I am extremely proud of you."

"If I could blush, I'd be doing that now," I say shyly, lowering my body and placing my right paw over my eye.

"I'm afraid that you won't see Buddy for a while," Saint Peter continues. "She has not completed her life's purpose yet. When she does, you will see her.

"But for now, you will get to meet people who knew Buddy from the generations that lived before her time. Wait until you see the look on Grandpa's face when he sees Buddy's mother; his wife. Oh, boy!" Saint Peter certainly is having fun with this idea.

"Grandpa would want to see me first though, right?" I say.

Saint Peter explains, "My precious dog, sometimes there will be a person that holds the Number One spot in the heart of a loved one. Not that Grandpa doesn't love you, but like Buddy comes first to you, his wife – Buddy's mother – comes first to him."

"That makes total sense to me. I apologize for being so self-centered." I reply.

"You are just excited and curious. Don't worry. Worries are for people who haven't arrived here yet. Your fears are gone. Once you go through this gate, you will never have troubles again."

I almost expect Saint Peter to put a blindfold on me and surprise me with what was coming next. This is more exciting than chasing a bunny rabbit.

Placing a pure gold collar around my neck and attaching a matching leash, Saint Peter says, "It is customary for me to walk you through the gate. I will announce your presence to everyone and then leave you free to roam and get familiar with your surroundings. After you walk and sniff for a while, the others—all creatures—will slowly begin to acquaint themselves with you."

I hesitate. "You will stay with me, right?"

"Eppy, dear heart, you need to do this on your own. You will be embraced and loved. You'll experience the true meaning of heaven." Saint Peter's face is so pure, not a line or a mark on it. His lips are dark in color, like a baby's.

"Besides, you will be seeing lots more of me. I will bring others here. I promise to have conversations with you to see how you're coming along. Relax." he says.

This is reassuring. My eagerness returns.

"Here we go! 1-2-3!"

The heavy gate slowly opens. I step inside and drop onto a soft floor in awe.

I turn my head from left to right; I see green trees, turquoise waters, long winding roads. The sky is blue with fluffy clouds. It is filled with people in rainbow printed hot air balloons. My new world is colorful, even more so than earth!

One by one, people and dogs (ok, some cats, too), and many other creatures come forward to welcome me. It will take eternity, literally, to meet them all. Saint Peter crouches down next to me and slowly removes my collar and leash.

"Eppy," Saint Peter says quietly, patting my head and letting me lean into him. "You won't have to meet everyone all at once. In a very short time, you will meet a creature that is connected to a loved one that hasn't arrived here yet. He or she will introduce themselves and tell you their connection to a creature that you knew in life."

With that said, Saint Peter stands, gives my head one last pat, turns and walks away. I watch as he goes back through the gate. Once he is gone from view, I turn back to my new world.

I was ready to begin.

A tall, quite elegant female approaches me. "Welcome, my name is Audrey. I used to be an actress."

She is followed by a jewel-like eyed toad who says, "Welcome, I entered here with no name, but now I am known as Wart."

This seems to go on forever, not that I understand "forever"any more.

A young woman with dark hair reaches for my paw and grasps it tightly. Smiling broadly, she says, "Eppy, I believe that we are connected."

"Really? Were you a dog once?" I am skeptical.

The woman laughs heartily. "No, I was never a dog. I have always been a woman. It's just that your two favorite humans are related to me. I am Grandpa's wife."

Okay, so Grandpa married a woman younger than Buddy? Was it too warm in here; did I overheat somehow?

Seeing my confused look, she smiles again, "You see, once you come here, you become young again. No pain and no worries."

"Since Grandpa is Buddy's father that means...." I stammer.

"Correct, I am Buddy's mother. My name is Paulita," She says, her eyes getting misty, but I know there are no tears here.

I am so excited that I run in circles and become totally dizzy and out of breath. Trying to sit still and regain at least a shred of composure (like that would happen), I begin firing questions:

"Are they alright? Do they miss me? Er...I know Grandpa misses you terribly. You have the 'number one' position in his heart. Speaking of being number one, is Buddy smiling again? You can tell me everything."

Just don't tell me they got another dog.

The mere thought stops me in my tracks. Then, I remember that emotions like jealousy and apprehension do not exist here.

Half-heartedly, I regain my composure, "Oh, just wanted you to know, I'll be okay if they got another dog. They must be lonesome without me."

Saint Peter, please give me strength, I plead to myself. *Does it take time for feelings like anxiety to dissipate?* I wonder?

"They are still too heartbroken; they knew they would never find another dog like you." she responds. Paulita is very solemn and sincere. I won't lie since it's not allowed here, but I think that feeling relief is permitted.

"What do we do from here?" I try to sound casual. Patience is a virtue and virtue is going to become my middle name.

"My dear dog (that sounds familiar), your mind is still noisy. You literally have eternity left and you will live here in the present. Soon you will not think of your past or worry about the future. Expectation will be removed from your mind and replaced with only loving thoughts of the here and now."

Embarrassed by my behavior, I lower my head in respect. "You are absolutely right. This is the most delightful place ever, and I am truly appreciative."

Paulita sits next to me and, just like Saint Peter had, she softly pats my head.

A mischievous look comes over her face.

"I'll tell you one thing just because you're a novice and don't know any better," She says playfully.

"Ok, thanks," I say. I try to act nonchalant.

Paulita exclaims, "We'll see Buddy and Grandpa again! I can't tell you the details, but I can guarantee that I am telling you the truth. Remember, we can't lie here."

Together we jump up and down, waving our arms/paws in the air. Paulita takes me to an ocean where we splash in waves, then run back to shore and take a deep breath of fresh, salty air.

We hike up a mountain and sit quietly in awe of the exquisiteness spread out before us. Paradise is open to *all* of God's creatures.

I feel, euphoric, blissful, joyous, elated—just downright happy as a clam. I hope that I will meet a clam here for that matter!

Dog-tired, I circle around three times and settle down in a soft spot on what looks like a cloud. I am totally convinced that food, then rest will soon be bestowed upon me.

There is one thing that I now knew for sure:

I am the luckiest dog not alive.

If there are no dogs in Heaven, then when I die I want to go where they went.

-Will Rogers

Eppylogue

Eppy spent his long days, eating, tooling around in the ocean, napping and philosophizing with Paulita about life (or whatever this was). The past was the past and this was now. Paulita was smart, but Eppy got to teach her something special. It was called "living in the moment."

"See that Milk Bone, Paulita?" he would demonstrate. "My attention is totally focused on that Milk Bone. One hundred percent focused. No other thought can cross my mind. Now, let's do an exercise."

Eppy placed a slice of Boston cream pie and a fork in front of Paulita. A little bird told him (ha-ha, another silly earthly expression; he loved these!) this was Paulita's favorite dessert. Boston cream pie is a cake, but that's not what's significant here.

"Try this pie, and tell me what you think," he instructed.

Paulita took one bite, closed her eyes and smiled.

"I taste sponge cake, a rich thick cream, and smooth delicious chocolate. Ah, chocolate!"

"Did you contemplate anything else while you were eating that pie…er, actually, cake?"

Paulita thought for just a moment.

"No, Eppy, I did not. My mind was focused only on that lovely dessert. Mesmerizing really. You have a knack for teaching others. Why not share your knowledge around here?"

Even Paulita hadn't figured out *exactly* where she was. However, it was obvious to every soul there that her heaven would need to include one more person.

Eppy became the most talented teacher on this topic, and as word spread, Saint Peter called upon him to teach this skill to all who entered through the gate. It was a large area to cover, this place of supreme bliss, but Eppy was determined to make an impression on those he encountered. With the help of several software engineers and Paulita's artistic expertise, Eppy managed to create a brilliant PowerPoint presentation entitled, "Eppy's Present."

With laptop in paw, Eppy traveled to wherever he was summoned.

Eppy lectures were spectacular, no doubt about it.

It was a gradual process, but Eppy eventually became the dog that he always hoped he would be.

Too bad Buddy isn't here to witness this firsthand, he would think, *but that's alright, I'll be even more perfect by the time she gets here. Wait—"more perfect" makes no sense. Guess I still have a journey ahead of me.*

His visits with Saint Peter became more sporadic. Eventually, he didn't see Saint Peter at all. *That's OK, someone needs him more than I do. We'll meet again when the time is right.*

That day would come sooner than Eppy anticipated; for all the wrong reasons.

One day Paulita came up to Eppy and said, "I need to speak with you about something."

I saw a frown on her face. We don't use gloomy facial expressions here! What could have happened? I'd panic but we don't do that here either.

"You can talk to me about anything, you know that," Eppy said tenderly.

"It's about my husband. You know, Grandpa. I'm worried about him. I think that something bad may have happened to him," Paulita said in a somewhat shaky voice.

Worry? Paulita is worrying? I don't even remember what that feels like. This is quite serious.

"But Paulita, Grandpa is with Buddy. He's fine, I'm certain, probably drinking his Manhattan and watching the Patriots game as we speak."

I liked that I understood things like football now. Having an enhanced brain had its advantages, Eppy mused.

"Eppy," Paulita panted almost like a dog, "Promise me you won't tell anyone about my anxiety."

"Fear is not allowed here. I'm frightened and I can't control my emotions. I'm just not able to stop these feelings of dread, Eppy!"

Paulita dropped to her knees, covered her eyes, and wept. Eppy pulled her into him, burrowing her face into his soft neck. He did not want a soul to overhear her sobs.

How can this even be possible? I should feel shock, but I don't even know how to experience that here! Logic is what I have been blessed with and here I go!

"Paulita, listen to me," Eppy said. "I want you to sit up straight and pretend you have a delicious piece of Boston cream…no, let's make it Key Lime pie in front of you. Concentrate."

She did as he instructed, sat back, and apologized. *Another thing we don't do here is apologize,* Eppy thought.

"It's going to be fine," Eppy said. "You wait here and I will go and find out where Grandpa is, okay?"

He smiled, hoping he sounded convincing. Paulita smiled back weakly and nodded. Eppy realized he had no other choice. He had to summon Saint Peter.

"Saint Peter, you haven't aged a day!" Eppy was elated by the sight of him.

"Oh, Eppy, you are such an amusing dog; always have been. You do realize that humor is my weakness – so to speak. Why, I even requested laugh lines for my face!"

"Now, Saint Peter, stop pulling my paw," Eppy grinned.

Pleasantries now over, they looked closely into each other's eyes. Saint Peter spoke first.

"I know why you're here," Saint Peter said solemnly. "It's about Paulita."

Eppy lowered his head. "Yes, Saint Peter."

"We do have what we refer to as a 'celestial glitch,' Eppy. It's rare because everyone finds peace and comfort here. No regrets or feelings of loneliness should exist here. God must know what causes this malfunction, but it's not something that has been shared with me."

"A 'celestial glitch'? Tell me this is a joke." If it was, Eppy wanted no part of it.

"Cheer up, Ep, I'm going to direct you to one of our RSC's. An acronym for 'resident spirit clairvoyant'. I have just the one for you. We'll get Paulita 'up to speed again' or whatever that expression is," Saint Peter was thinking hard about this. I could see wheels spinning above his forehead.

Eppy followed Saint Peter, stopping briefly as he encountered his old friends.

Willy was Meg's dog; he and Buddy used to run with them around a lake that he now knew was called Quannapowitt. Talk about a mouthful. Eppy also saw Judy's cat, Tuffy. They had a great laugh together.

"You were one heck of a nuisance in my home," Tuffy recollected. "Can't believe Judy would let you into the house and then you'd proceed to eat all three bowls of cat food. And everyone thought it was a riot! Plus, Judy had an entire cabinet of dog treats just for you! She bought the expensive kind; Buddy let her spoil you."

"Good to see you too, pal," Eppy retorted, amused. "I'm sure at some point the crowd will be up here jogging around." *Maybe you and Willy can join them. I'm certain that I won't be running.* Eppy hadn't changed completely. Physical exertion was not any more appealing to him now than it had been back then.

Saint Peter and Eppy loved these little meet and greets. This was a mission, however, and in a determined manner, they continued with their search. It wasn't long before they met a gentle looking RSC. It was a woman and she was barely three feet tall. Her nose was large, as were her feet and hands. The woman's skin was wrinkled and rough.

Eppy tried not to stare at her, especially at her orange colored hair that stood high above her head, coming to a point at the top.

Eppy remembered the expression "Beauty is in the eye of the beholder" and realized that she was indeed lovely.

Saint Peter smiled warmly (didn't he always?) and introduced Eppy to Helga.

"Eppy," he explained, "Helga is a troll from Scandinavia. Trolls were considered Nordic fantasies and were categorized as monsters. Of course, that was make-believe, but what is true is that trolls were given supernatural powers. Due to that, we chose trolls to be our clairvoyants. Plus, Grandpa was of Scandinavian descent, thus our decision to converse with Helga. Do you understand?"

Eppy nodded, "Yes, Saint Peter. Helga, please proceed."

Helga looked straight past them and spoke, "Grandpa is not at his house. Buddy is there with the man you call 'Alpha Boy,' and they are enjoying dinner in the dining room. Grandpa's chair is empty, but neither of them look gloomy. I suspect Grandpa has been away for a while."

Her attention now focused back on Saint Peter, Helga queried, "You haven't seen him around here?"

Saint Peter nudged Eppy and replied, "Not unless he was wearing an invisible cloak and snuck in behind me somehow."

A pathetic attempt at humor, Eppy thought and wanted to say, *stick to your day job.*

"Well, he can't be too far away," Helga shrugged. "I just can't spot him."

"Thanks anyway, Helga," Saint Peter said, "he'll show up." Eppy nodded, put his paw in Saint Peter's hand and they walked away.

"Saint Peter," Eppy said. "Do you think the reason Grandpa is missing is that Paulita had this…. attack, and her husband had to possibly wait 'outside' until she recuperated?"

Saint Peter did not respond immediately. They continued to walk, nodding and waving to divine souls as they strolled.

"Eppy," Saint Peter said without slowing down his pace. "You are spot on about Paulita. Until she can recover from her celestial glitch, your Grandpa will not show up here."

Eppy took this as a challenge.

"I have a strategy, Saint Peter. Don't you worry your handsome little head over the situation, then thought, *I think I am being totally irreverent.*

"Ok, my witty and self-assured dog, Paulita is all yours. Send me a message if you need my help. I doubt you will." Saint Peter winked and walked away with a wave of his hand.

Paulita was alone, and her face was expressionless. When she spotted Eppy, she gave a feeble wave as Eppy thought, *this reminds me of the last tail wag I gave to Buddy. Not acceptable at all. I need to take control of this situation, with tender loving care (TLC as I've learned to say up here, or perhaps over here? Still a bit confused myself.)*

"Paulita," Eppy exclaimed. "You look GREAT! Did you change your hair? Different color lipstick perhaps? I like that dress; it highlights your emerald green eyes."

Paulita forced a smile. "I know what you're doing, my faithful friend. Thank you. Going for a jog which should make me feel better."

"Well, whatever you're doing, it's working. Wait until Grand…. Okay, well, bye, have fun. See you later, alligator," Eppy would have been perspiring if that were at all possible.

Eppy had to think quick; he didn't want Paulita to jog away from him. It was time for Eppy to have a serious talk with her. He composed himself and looked up at her. She acknowledged his stern look and waited for him to say something.

"Sit down and sit still, Paulita," Eppy said. Paulita did as she was told. "Please tell me what you have learned here."

Forced to listen to him, she responded, "Well, I've learned that this is a physical paradise and that there are no health issues here and that if you wait patiently, astonishing events will occur."

She paused and repeated, "Astonishing events will occur, astonishing…. events…. will …. occur."

"Eppy," her face lit up like a dog who had just spotted a squirrel. "I have been so stupid. Oh, no, not stupid because we are not *stupid* here. Did something go wrong with my wiring, do you suppose? Is that even possible?"

Eppy grinned from ear to ear. He loved doing this now that he had sparkling teeth (His earthly teeth were cracked and broken in many spots from when he tried to break through that horrible crate he had once been stuck in.)

"I never thought you were stupid," said a male voice from behind her. "In my opinion, you're the smartest and most beautiful woman in all the heavens."

Paulita closed her eyes and smiled before she slowly turned around.

It took Eppy a few seconds to realize who this man was. He was still piecing things together here; it was a progression.

"And I suppose you've been looking at women all over the heavens while I've been here fretting?" she said. *No more tears.*

Grandpa just smiled, patted Eppy on the head and said, "Good boy, Ep." Then Grandpa gave him a Milk Bone and took Paulita in his arms.

Mission accomplished, the luckiest dog not alive circled around three times and plopped down, just like he had always done after Grandpa gave him a treat.

Acknowledgements

I would like to express my gratitude to the following for their tremendous support:

I owe my colleagues at the Gloucester Writers Center an extraordinary debt. Without Barbara Boudreau, Dan Duffy, Stacey Dexter, Jane Keddy, John Mullen, and Cindy Schimanski, I could never have made it to "The Finish Line."

Thank you to Terri Weber Mangos for introducing me to the group.

Special thanks to Sandra Williams for her unending support, editing assistance, and humor.

If Don Gibbon had not been placed into my life (thanks Di Barry), I wouldn't have illustrations that depicted Eppy's personality so perfectly. If there are saints, Donnie is one of them.

Speaking of saints, my book cover designer, Xavier Bertolotti, has the patience of one. Xavier went above and beyond.

My thanks to Jim Masciarelli for introducing me to the Sanibel Island Writers' Conference; for Felicia Tavilla for hosting me.

I am obliged to my brother, Michael Hendrickson, for being my #1 dog walker. He was always there when I needed him and had many memorable adventures with Eppy.

Who could get anything accomplished without the help of friends? They are too numerous to name here, and for that I count my blessings.

In remembrance of David Carlson; we shared a love of Gloucester, our Finnish heritage, and our "unique" sense of humor. Thank you for showing me the beauty of Lake Superior and teaching me the true meaning of *Sisu*.

My love to Brian who, despite knowing that I was entirely untrainable, brought me home with him anyway.

"Saving one dog will not change the world, but surely for that one dog, the world will change forever."

-Karen Davison

With Respect and Appreciation to the Following:

Pawsafe Animal Rescue, where I "rescued" Eppy at their adoption event in Belmont, MA. It's organizations like this who diligently endeavor to see that every animal has a loving, responsible home, free from anguish and abandonment.

The Cape Ann Veterinary and Bethel, Maine animal hospitals for their care of Eppy. These wonderful professionals also comforted me when the inevitable occurred.

Cape Ann Animal Aid. Our local shelter is a non-profit, no kill organization committed to hard work and enhancing the quality of the pets they attend to, and then place into caring homes.

The Luckiest Dog Not Alive is on Amazon

For additional information and to order books, please write to:
suvetarpublications@gmail.com

"Grandpa"

Made in the USA
Columbia, SC
04 March 2018